PATHWAY BIBLE GUIDES

Church Matters

1 CORINTHIANS 1-7

BY BRYSON SMITH

GW00503812

matthiasmedia

Church Matters
Pathway Bible Guides: 1 Corinthians 1-7
© Matthias Media 2006

Matthias Media
(St Matthias Press Ltd. ACN 067 558 365)
PO Box 225
Kingsford NSW 2032
Australia
Telephone: (02) 9663 1478; international: +61-2-9663-1478
Facsimile: (02) 9663 3265; international: +61-2-9663-3265
Email: info@matthiasmedia.com.au
Internet: www.matthiasmedia.com.au

Unless otherwise indicated, all Scripture quotations are from The Holy Bible, English Standard Version, copyright © 2001 by Crossway Bibles, a division of Good News Publishers. Used by permission. All rights reserved.

ISBN 1 921068 52 3

All rights reserved. Except as may be permitted by the Copyright Act, no part of this publication may be reproduced in any form or by any means without prior permission from the publisher.

Cover design and typesetting by Lankshear Design Pty Ltd.

CONTENTS

BEFORE YOU BEGIN

Church can evoke different feelings for different people. For some, church is boring, stifling and full of awkward people. For others, church is wonderful; they can't wait to jump out of bed on a Sunday to be with their church family.

Whatever we may feel about church, it's important that our behaviour and attitudes are shaped by the way God feels about church. 1 Corinthians is a very helpful book because it shows us how precious church is to God and therefore how we should treat it with great care.

At one level, it's a bit strange to be looking at this subject in 1 Corinthians because out of all the first-century churches mentioned in the New Testament, you'd be hard-pressed to find one as troubled as the church at Corinth. It was fractured by factions and divisions. It suffered from elitism and open hostility, with members taking each other to court. The rich looked down on the poor and ignored their needs. People were indulging in sexual immorality, with one congregation member having sex with his stepmother without qualms. There were those who were getting drunk at church meals. There were those who were bickering over spiritual gifts in the church. During meetings, prophets would leap up with a 'word from the Lord' while others would leap up to speak in tongues, much to the irritation of those who weren't into those sort of things. In addition, even though Paul was the founder of their church

(Acts 18), the Corinthians didn't seem to think much of him and his 'foolish' message!

Yet despite their flaws and difficulties, Paul still described the church at Corinth as precious and blessed, for it was no less than the church *of God* (1:2). The Corinthian Christians have been cleansed, sanctified and justified, enriched with the blessings of God's grace, endowed with every spiritual gift and brought into the fellowship of Jesus Christ. Their new identity as God's people could not help but change the way they relate to one another and the world—particularly as they gathered together before God.

Is this how you view yourself? Is this how you view your church?

In these studies, we'll work through the first seven chapters of 1 Corinthians and take a closer look at all the different 'church matters' that Paul raises with the congregation he fathered. It is my prayer that as you learn more about how God views his church, you will grow in your appreciation of what it means to be part of it, and in turn understand how it is to be valued. For church really does matter!

Bryson Smith
June 2006

1. GOD'S CHURCH

1 Corinthians 1:1-17

 Getting started

What thoughts, feelings and/or images does the word 'church' produce in you? Why?

 **Light from the Word**

Read 1 Corinthians 1:1-9.

1. Who is this letter written to? Who is it from? How are they each described in verses 1-2?

2. List all the things that God has done for the Corinthian church (vv. 4-9).

3. Do you think these things are true of every church? If so, to what extent?

Read 1 Corinthians 1:10-12.

4. What problem does Paul describe here?

5. How do you think this problem may have arisen?

6. Do you think this can still be a problem in churches today?

Read 1 Corinthians 1:13-17.

7. What seems to be Paul's main point in these verses?

8. What effect do you think this should have on the divisions and quarrelling in the church?

9. In verses 4-9, Paul reminds the church of the abundant blessings they have in Christ. What effect do you think this should have on the divisions and quarrelling in the church?

10. In the coming studies, we will see that the Corinthian church had lots of problems. Why do you think Paul chose this particular problem to tackle first?

 ## To finish

Compare your 'Getting started' answer to your answer for Question 2. Are there any attitudes or behaviours towards your own church that you need to change?

 ## Give thanks and pray

Give thanks for the church family which you are a part of. Ask God to protect your church from quarrelling and destructive gossip.

2. POWER IN GOD'S CHURCH

1 Corinthians 1:17-2:5

 Getting started

Why is it that we are sometimes embarrassed to talk about Jesus Christ and his death on the cross? How much of our difficulty has to do with the message itself?

💡 Light from the Word

Read 1 Corinthians 1:17-2:5.

1. According to 1:17-19, what is it that saves people?

2. In what sense does the gospel message seem 'foolish' and 'weak' (1:18-22)?

3. What did the Jews of Paul's time find more impressive than the gospel (1:22-25)?

4. What did the Greeks of Paul's time find more impressive than the gospel (1:22-25)?

5. Look back over the previous two answers. Are there things which people today find more impressive than the gospel? Are there things which people sometimes add to the gospel to make it seem more impressive?

6. How does the composition of the Corinthian church illustrate the fact that it is the message of the cross alone which saves people (1:26-31)?

7. How does Paul's own behaviour testify to the fact that it's the message of the cross which saves people (2:1-5)?

8. When Paul says that his message and preaching were done "in demonstration of the Spirit and of power", what sort of power does he have mind? (Look back at 1:17-18.)

9. Paul emphasizes that it is the gospel alone which saves people. What effect do you think this should have on the divisions and quarrelling in the church?

 ## To finish

"When we tell someone about Jesus, we don't need to be clever, just clear." Is that statement a good summary for this study? Why/why not? Is this an encouragement for you in your personal evangelism? Why/why not?

 ## Give thanks and pray

Pray for specific people whom you have opportunity to share the gospel with. Ask for courage, and confidence in the gospel message.

3. WISDOM IN GOD'S CHURCH

....

1 Corinthians 2:6-16

 **Getting started**

What words would you use to describe the Holy Spirit?

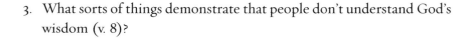

Light from the Word

Read 1 Corinthians 2:6-16.

1. In verses 6-10, Paul compares the wisdom of the world with the wisdom of the gospel. How is God's wisdom different from the wisdom of this age?

2. Why are "secret" and "hidden" good words to describe God's wisdom?

3. What sorts of things demonstrate that people don't understand God's wisdom (v. 8)?

4. If God's wisdom is secret, how can we come to know it (vv. 10-12)?

5. What is the significance of the use of the word "freely" in verse 12?

6. Try to write out verse 13 in your own words.

7. When it comes to understanding God's wisdom, how does the person without the Spirit contrast with the spiritual person (vv. 14-16)?

8. What do you think verses 15-16 mean?

9. What implications does this passage have for the quarrels and factions that exist in the Corinthian church?

 **To finish**

What implications does this study have concerning the importance of prayer?

 Give thanks and pray

Give thanks for the wonderful gift of God's Spirit. Pray that the Spirit will provide you with insight into the thoughts of God himself.

4. LEADERSHIP IN GOD'S CHURCH

1 Corinthians 3

 Getting started

What do you think are the characteristics of a good leader?

☀ Light from the Word

Read 1 Corinthians 3:1-4.

1. Paul describes the Corinthians as not "spiritual" but "of the flesh, as infants in Christ" (v. 1). Why?

Read 1 Corinthians 3:5.

2. What image does Paul use to describe Christian leadership in verse 5?

3. What seems to be the main lesson from this image?

Read 1 Corinthians 3:6-8.

4. What image does Paul use here to describe Christian leadership?

5. What seems to be the main lesson from this image?

Read 1 Corinthians 3:9-15.

6. What image does Paul use here to describe Christian leadership?

7. What seems to be the main lesson from this image?

Read 1 Corinthians 3:16-23.

8. How does Paul describe the church? (See also v. 9.)

9. What does this mean for the preciousness of God's church (v. 17)?

10. What effect should this have on 'boasting in men' (v. 21)? Why?

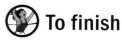 To finish

How does this chapter affect your view of ministry in your church?

 Give thanks and pray

Thank God for the leaders of your church. Pray for them using the truths you've discovered in this study as a guide.

5. FAITHFULNESS IN GOD'S CHURCH

1 Corinthians 4

 Getting started

When do you find it hardest to be faithful to God? How can we help each other during these times?

💡 Light from the Word

Read 1 Corinthians 4:1-2. Note that verse 1 summarizes some of Paul's main points from chapters 2 and 3—that leaders are Christ's servants who declare God's 'foolish' wisdom of Christ crucified.

1. Who do you think are the "us" that Paul refers to in verse 1?

2. What does God require of those whom he entrusts with a duty (v. 2)?

Read 1 Corinthians 4:3-7.

3. According to verses 3-5, whose opinion about whether we have been trustworthy matters most? Why?

4. In what sense did Paul and Apollos exemplify not going "beyond what is written" (v. 6)?

5. How were the Corinthians guilty of going "beyond what is written" (v. 7)?

Read 1 Corinthians 4:8-21.

6. In the table below, list the words which Paul uses in verses 8-13 to describe the Corinthians, and the words he uses to describe himself. In the eyes of the world, which would be judged as being more successful: Paul or the Corinthians?

Corinthians	Paul

7. Why does Paul make this comparison (vv. 14-15)?

8. What does Paul want the Corinthians to do? What has he done to help them achieve this (vv. 16-17)?

9. What is Paul hoping to avoid? Why (vv. 18-21)?

 ## To finish

At the end of this chapter, Paul finishes addressing the problem of quarrelling and boasting in the Corinthian church. Look back over the previous four studies and list some of the comforts and challenges that God has been raising with you in his word and by his Spirit.

 ## Give thanks and pray

Use the previous question as a guide for giving thanks to God.

6. JUDGEMENT IN GOD'S CHURCH

1 Corinthians 5:1-6:8

 **Getting started**

"God is a killjoy. He's just anti-sex." How would you respond to this sort of comment?

💡 Light from the Word

Read 1 Corinthians 5:1-5.

1. What new issue does Paul now address? What specific incident has prompted Paul to raise this issue?

2. What has been the church's reaction so far? How does Paul feel about this?

3. What does Paul want the church to do?

Verse 5 is a difficult one. What does it mean to hand someone over to Satan? The context (v. 2) suggests that this is probably referring to being publicly expelled from the church. In the New Testament, the world outside the church is seen as the realm of Satan. To be expelled from Christ's household is to be delivered into the region where Satan roams and holds sway. Paul offers three reasons for taking this drastic step.

Reason 1 (5:5)

Re-read 1 Corinthians 5:5.

4. What reason does Paul give for expelling this man from the church?

5. Public discipline is always a very serious matter. How can this be seen as actually a loving act?

Reason 2 (5:6-11)

Read 1 Corinthians 5:6-11.

6. What reason does Paul give for expelling this man from the church?

7. Why do you think it is more serious to "associate" with immoral people in the church than with immoral people in the community?

Reason 3 (5:12-6:8)

Read 1 Corinthians 5:12-6:8.

8. Who are the "saints" and what are they going to do?

9. If the "saints" are going to judge the world, why is it inappropriate to take each other to civil courts?

10. If the "saints" are going to judge the world, why is it therefore inappropriate that they are not judging the immoral brother mentioned in 5:1ff?

 ## To finish

How does this passage show us again that church is very precious to God?

Give thanks and pray

Thank God that his church is so precious and valuable. Pray that you would value your church family as much as God does.

7. PURITY IN GOD'S CHURCH

....

1 Corinthians 6:9-20

 Getting started

Which do you consider more important: what you think with your mind or what you do with your body?

Light from the Word

Read 1 Corinthians 6:9-11.

1. In verses 9-10, Paul mentions the kinds of people who will not inherit the kingdom of God. Why do you think he warns against being deceived about this (v. 9)?

2. "And such were some of you", says Paul in verse 11. What is now different about the Corinthians?

Read 1 Corinthians 6:12-20.

3. "All things are lawful for me" is probably a quote from some in the church who felt that they were above moral rules and that their bodies had nothing to do with their spiritual lives. Using your own words, fill in the following sentences to discover the ways in which Paul refutes this idea:

Verse 12: "All things are lawful for me"— BUT _____

Verse 12: "All things are lawful for me"— BUT _____

4. "Food is meant for the stomach and the stomach for food" (v. 13) may also be a quote from some in the church who thought that since God is going to destroy the physical world, then what we do physically doesn't matter. What two reasons does Paul give to show that the relationship between food and the stomach is different from the relationship between our bodies and sexual immorality?

Reason 1 (v. 13): _____

Reason 2 (v. 14): _____

5. What does Paul mean by the statement, "your bodies are members of Christ"? (Hint: take a peek at 1 Cor 12:27.)

6. What implication does being "members of Christ" have on sexual immorality (vv. 15-17)?

7. How is sexual immorality different to other sins?

8. Verses 19-20 are sometimes quoted by people to argue that we should exercise, eat properly and not smoke. Do you think this is a fair use of these verses?

9. How is this section a suitable conclusion to the problem which Paul first raised in 1 Corinthians 5:1?

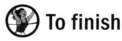 ## To finish

What specific and practical things can you do to "flee from sexual immorality"?

 ## Give thanks and pray

Thank God for the washing, sanctifying, justifying work of Jesus Christ by the Spirit of God. Pray about your answer to the last question, especially in specific areas of your life where you may be strongly tempted by sexual immorality.

8. GODLINESS IN GOD'S CHURCH

....
1 Corinthians 7

 **Getting started**

Which does our society say is better: being single or being married?

💡 Light from the Word

Read 1 Corinthians 7:1.

1. Why does Paul now raise the issue of marriage and singleness?

2. "Chapter 7 is like listening to one side of a telephone conversation." How does verse 1 confirm this statement? What care should we therefore take when reading these verses?

This is a confusing chapter in some respects. It often seems like Paul is jumping from one topic to the next. In order to examine the main idea that unites the whole chapter, we'll look at it under the three main truths that Paul wants to convey.

Truth 1: Marriage is good

Read 1 Corinthians 7:1-16.

3. In verses 2-9, what does Paul say are the advantages of being married? How does this tie in to the previous topic of the letter (6:18-20)?

4. After talking about sexual relations in marriage, Paul immediately goes on to talk about the permanency of marriage in a range of situations (vv. 10-16). Why do you think his emphasis on the permanency of marriage is so important?

Truth 2: Singleness is good

Read 1 Corinthians 7:25-40.

5. What advantages does Paul see in being single?

6. What do you think Paul means by "the present distress" (v. 26)?

7. What seems to be Paul's main point in verses 29-35?

Truth 3: Remain in your situation

Read 1 Corinthians 7:17-24.

8. What "rule" does Paul spell out in this section (v. 17)?

9. How does Paul illustrate this "rule"?

10. What relevance does this have to the question of whether or not to get married?

 ## To finish

Often we blame our circumstances for our problems. How is 1 Corinthians 7 a good corrective? Are you using your life circumstances as an excuse to be ungodly?

 ## Give thanks and pray

Skim back over the studies in this book and pick out the truths which highlight the value and importance of church. Use them as the basis for prayer.

FOR THE LEADER

What are Pathway Bible Guides?

The Pathway Bible Guides aim to provide simple, straightforward Bible study material for:

- Christians who are new to studying the Bible (perhaps because they've been recently converted or because they have joined a Bible study group for the first time);
- Christians who find other studies[1] too much of a stretch.

Accordingly, we've designed the studies to be short, straightforward and easy to use, with a simple vocabulary. At the same time, we've tried to do justice to the passages being studied, and to model good Bible-reading principles. We've tried to be simple without being simplistic; no-nonsense without being no-content.

The questions and answers assume a small group context, but it should be easy to adapt them to suit different situations, such as individual study and one-to-one.

Your role as leader

Because many in your group may not be used to reading and discussing a Bible passage in a group context, a greater level of responsibility will fall to you as the leader of the discussions. There are the usual responsibilities of preparation, prayer and managing group dynamics. In addition, there will be an extra dimension of forming and encouraging good Bible reading habits in people who may not have much of an idea of what those habits look like.

Questions have been kept deliberately brief and simple. For this reason, you may have to fill in some of the gaps that may have been addressed in, say, an Interactive Bible Study. Such 'filling in' may take the form of asking follow-up questions, or using your best judgement to work out when you might need to

---

1. Such as the Interactive Bible Study (IBS) series also available from Matthias Media.

supply background information. That sort of information, and some suggestions about other questions you could ask, may be found in the following leader's notes. In addition, a *New Bible Dictionary* is always a useful aid to preparation, and simple commentaries such as those in the *Tyndale* or *Bible Speaks Today* series are often helpful. Consult them after you have done your own preparation.

On the question of background information, these studies are written from the assumption that God's word stands alone. God works through his Holy Spirit and the leaders he has gifted—such as you—to make his meaning clear. Assuming this to be true, the best interpreter and provider of background information for Scripture will not be academic historical research, but Scripture itself. Extra historical information may be useful for the purpose of illustration, but it is unnecessary for understanding and applying what God says to us.

The format of the studies

The discussion questions on each passage follow a simple pattern. There is a question at the beginning of each discussion that is intended to get people talking around the issues raised by the passage, and to give you some idea of how people are thinking. If the group turns out to be confident, motivated and comfortable with each other and the task at hand, you may even decide to skip this question. Alternatively, if the group members are shy or quiet, you may decide to think of related types of questions that you could add in to the study, so as to maintain momentum in a non-threatening way.

After the first question, the remaining questions work through the passage sequentially, alternating between observation, interpretation and application in a way that will become obvious when you do your own preparation. The final question of each discussion, just before the opportunity for prayer, could be used in some groups to encourage (say) one person each week to give a short talk (it could be 1 minute or 5 minutes, depending on the topic and the people). The thinking here is that there's no better way to encourage understanding of a passage than to get people to the point where they can explain it to others. Use your judgement in making best use of this final exercise each week, depending on the people in your group.

In an average group, it should be possible to work through the study in approximately 45 minutes. But it's important that you work out what your group is capable of, given the time available, and make adjustments accordingly. Work out in advance which questions or sub-points can be omitted if time is short. And have a few supplementary questions or discussion starters up your sleeve if your group is dealing with the material quickly and hungering for more. Each group is different. It's your job as leader to use the printed material as 'Bible *Guides*', and not as a set of questions that you must rigidly stick to regardless of your circumstances.

Preparation: 60/40/20

Ideally, group members should spend half an hour reading over the passage and pencilling in some answers *before* they come to the group. Not every group member will do this, of course, but encourage them with the idea that the more they prepare for the study, the more they will get out of the discussion.

In terms of your own preparation as leader, we recommend you put aside approximately *two hours*, either all at once or in two one-hour blocks, and that you divide up the time as follows:

- 60 minutes reading the passage and answering the questions yourself as best you can (without looking at the leader's notes or Bible commentaries);
- 40 minutes consulting the leader's notes (plus other resources, like commentaries). Add to your own answers, and jot down supplementary questions or other information that you want to have available as you lead the discussion. Make sure you write everything you need on the study pages—the last thing you want to do is to keep turning to the 'answers' in the back during the group discussion;
- 20 minutes praying about the study and for your group members.

This 60/40/20 pattern will help you to focus on the Bible and what it's saying, rather than simply regurgitating to the group what is in the leader's notes. Remember, these notes are just that—notes to offer some help and guidance. They are not the Bible! As a pattern of preparation, 60/40/20 also helps you to keep praying for yourself and your group, that God would give spiritual growth as his word is sown in your hearts (see Luke 8:4-15; 1 Cor 3:5-7).

If, for some reason, you have less or more time to spend in preparation, simply apply the 60/40/20 proportions accordingly.

1. GOD'S CHURCH

1 Corinthians 1:1-17

▶ Remember: 60/40/20

 Getting started

Hopefully the opening 'Getting started' question will prompt people to consider their own attitudes to church. This should provide a good jumping-off point into the study as we don't have to go far into 1 Corinthians before we discover some pretty remarkable truths about what the church means to God, and therefore what church should mean to us.

Studying the passage

At first glance, Paul's opening to 1 Corinthians is nothing out of the ordinary. There is the standard identification of who is writing (v. 1) and who the letter is going to (v. 2). There is also Paul's characteristic way of defining everyone (including himself) in terms of Jesus Christ (question 1).

However, what makes Paul's opening quite extraordinary is the way he describes the church at Corinth. At one level, the church is a mess—plagued with divisiveness, quarrelling, elitism, hostility, inequality, sexual immorality, debauchery and confusion. Yet despite all these difficulties, Paul still describes it as precious and blessed. Question 2 should help highlight the fact that, among other things, the Corinthians have been sanctified and are called to be saints (v. 2), they have been enriched in every way (v. 5), they do not lack any spiritual gift (v. 7) and they have been called into fellowship with Jesus Christ (v. 9). These are remarkable affirmations, given the problems which exist in the church. It shows that despite its imperfections, the church at Corinth—the church of *God*—is still precious and blessed (v. 2).

Because the church is so precious to God, Paul doesn't waste any time before addressing some of its difficulties. The first issue that Paul decides to tackle in the letter is the problem of factions: the way that certain pressure groups have developed around personalities (vv. 11-12).

Paul states that he has heard that factions have developed around himself, Apollos, Cephas and even Christ (v. 12). He does not say that any of these men have fostered such factions; certainly Paul himself hasn't! Nor does he explain what it was about these people that caused others to gather around them. But we can hazard a pretty good guess as to the reason (question 5). Paul's following was perhaps bolstered by the fact that he was the founder of the church; he was the first one to evangelize the city and loyalty to him may well have developed because of that (Acts 18). Apollos, who came to Corinth and taught after Paul, was a very gifted speaker who had brought with him a strong Greek influence, for he was very learned in Greek philosophy (Acts 18:24ff). 'Cephas' is the Apostle Peter's Aramaic name, and the use of it here may be an indication that Peter's Jewishness had attracted a following. And then there was the Christ party—a group of people who may have been tired of all the other groups and who may have smugly said something along the lines of, "Look, we belong to Jesus, not any human teacher". Technically this was a good thing to say but it was probably said in a superior, divisive, competitive way.

Whatever the precise details, the church was split into sections. What had started as an inclination towards a personal preference had now deepened into judgementalism and factionalism. The battle lines were now drawn.

So how does Paul respond to this? His response extends right through into chapter 4 (Study 5) but in this study, we should be able to grasp two important points. Firstly, Paul reminding the church of their abundance in Christ (vv. 4-9) will, no doubt, help them to put their divisiveness into perspective (question 9). If, through Christ, the church already has every single thing God considers valuable, why split the church over trivial issues of ministry style?

Secondly, after acknowledging the existence of unseemly factions in the church, Paul immediately points the Corinthians to the fact that they share a common saviour (vv. 13-17; questions 7 and 8). Christ was crucified for them and they were baptized into his name. Divisiveness in a church family should therefore be smothered on the basis of the solidarity we share in following Christ.

There may be several reasons why Paul chooses to pick this problem as the first one he deals with (question 10). Perhaps he wants to clear the matter up quickly because his own name is implicated (v. 12). Maybe he perceives that there is no threat to God's church more serious than that of leadership squabbles. More likely, though, Paul targets this issue first because the matter highlights a serious flaw in the Corinthians' understanding of the gospel. (This will be drawn out further in Studies 2 and 3.)

To finish

Some time ago, I noticed a story on the news about the auction of one of John Lennon's guitars. It sold for a huge amount of money. I found this curious because the guitar looked as if it had been knocked around a lot. It was covered in scratches and dents. Yet despite its imperfections, it was precious because of the one it had belonged to.

How much more is this true of the church of God?

The church at Corinth certainly seems to have been knocked around a lot. It has lots and lots of problems. Yet despite its imperfections, it is the church of God in Corinth, and therefore it is precious beyond imagination and ought to be treated as such. Indeed, every church should be.

2. POWER IN GOD'S CHURCH

1 Corinthians 1:17-2:5

▶ Remember: 60/40/20

 ## Getting started

In this study, the Apostle Paul continues to address the problem of divisiveness within the Corinthian church. In the last study, we learnt that church factions should be smothered because of the riches we all enjoy in Christ and the unity we share in following Christ. Paul now adds another reason to this list: the very nature of the gospel message. Hopefully the 'Getting started' question will help people to start reflecting on this.

Studying the passage

Paul's opening point is straightforward. God uses the message of the cross of Christ to save people. By hearing the good news of Christ crucified for our sins, men and women called by God enter into his kingdom. In the words of Paul, the gospel message is therefore "the power of God" to those who are being saved (vv. 17-18; question 1).

To the world, however, the gospel seems strange and 'foolish'. Telling people about a Jew who was publicly executed 2,000 years ago can certainly seem like an irrelevant and pointless task (question 2). The apparent foolishness of the gospel tempts us to underestimate its power and to look for something more impressive. Paul refers to two groups who were doing just that: the Jews and the Greeks.

The Jews of Paul's time chased after miracles. The gospel accounts are full of numerous incidents in which the Jews urged Jesus to impress them with another miracle. They wanted spectacular acts of power. To them, the gospel message seemed mundane, weak and unexciting (v. 22; question 3).

The Greeks, on the other hand, were attracted to sophisticated and wise speech, and clever philosophy. To them, the gospel message seemed foolish and simplistic (v. 22; question 4).

Paul, however, saw the danger of both miracles and wise speech: they draw attention to themselves and feed the misperception that God's power is in them. But it is not; God's power and wisdom is in the message of the cross (vv. 23-25). He emphasizes this point by using both the Corinthian church (1:26-31) and himself (2:1-5) as examples which prove that it is the gospel which is the true power of God.

a) The example of the Corinthian church (1:26-31)

The Corinthians were not saved by being powerful, impressive people. They were not saved by being smarter than anyone else in Corinth. They were not saved by being socially more important than anyone else in Corinth. They were saved when they heard the gospel and responded to it. The message of Jesus brought them into the kingdom (question 6).

b) The example of Paul (2:1-5)

Paul deliberately chose not to be clever in his speech. He actively decided to do nothing more than preach the gospel so that when people responded in repentance and faith, it was clear that it wasn't the result of clever, persuasive words, but of God's power working through the message of Jesus crucified (question 7).

Question 8 is designed to double-check that Paul's example is clearly understood. When read out of context, Paul's description of his message and preaching as a "demonstration of the Spirit and of power" can sound like the exact opposite of what he intends. Many people immediately associate this sort of demonstration with spectacular, extraordinary events. However, Paul has already defined what he means by God's power: it is the message of the cross (1:17-18). Therefore, describing his preaching as a "demonstration of the Spirit and of power" is another way of Paul saying that his preaching was nothing more than "Jesus Christ and him crucified" (2:2). So Paul's behaviour was clear testimony to the fact that it is the message of the cross alone which saves people.

The final question is an important one for understanding this passage within the flow of the whole letter. Paul's discussion of the message of the cross has been prompted by the existence of divisions within the church. In this study Paul's argument has been that such divisions are pointless and indeed betray a misunderstanding of the gospel. Miracles never saved anyone. Clever speeches never saved anyone. It is the gospel which is the power of God. Divisions over personalities and styles of ministry should therefore cease.

To finish

Even though the original context of the verses covered in this study is divisiveness in the Corinthian church, this passage also has implications for our personal evangelism. When we next lean across the fence and tell our neighbour about Jesus, the power of God will be at work. When we have friends around for dinner and we start to share with them what Jesus has done for us through his death on the cross, we'll be unleashing the power of God. God's power doesn't depend on us being gifted speakers, or having clever and persuasive arguments. It simply depends on us faithfully sharing the apparently foolish message of "Jesus Christ and him crucified" (2:2).

3. WISDOM IN GOD'S CHURCH

1 Corinthians 2:6-16

▶ Remember: 60/40/20

 Getting started

This study covers important teaching about the role and ministry of God's Spirit. This is an area of confusion for many Christians, so the opening question is designed to help individuals reflect on what they do (or don't) know about the Holy Spirit.

Studying the passage

In the previous study, Paul stressed that people can only be saved through the gospel. Seeing miracles and hearing clever speeches doesn't save anyone. It is through the simple gospel message of Christ crucified that God delights to bring individuals into the kingdom of his Son. In this study, Paul continues to press this point. Not only is the gospel the power of God for salvation, it is also only through God's Spirit that we can come to understand the gospel. Paul explains this in two steps:

Step 1: The gospel is the hidden wisdom of God

In 1 Corinthians 2:6-9, Paul describes God's wisdom (i.e. the gospel of Christ; cf. 1 Cor 1:24) as "hidden" and "secret" from humanity. The stress here is twofold. Firstly, God's wisdom is different to the wisdom of this world in that it doesn't seem to be wisdom to the rulers of this age (question 1). It is for this reason that the rulers of Paul's age crucified Jesus (v. 8; question 3). Secondly (and more importantly to Paul's argument), the fact that God's wisdom is hidden means that man by his own efforts cannot discover God. Search as we might, God's wisdom is out of the scope of human wisdom (question 2).

Step 2: God has revealed his hidden wisdom through his Spirit

The truth that God's wisdom is hidden and secret would be terrible on its own; humanity would be left without hope of ever really knowing our Creator. Verse 10, however, contains some wonderfully good news: God in his goodness has revealed his wisdom through his own Spirit, in much the same way that a human person can be known when that person choices to reveal and share themselves (question 4).

Imagine a game of hide-and-seek where you can't find the person hiding. You've worked out all these theories about where they are and why they would choose this place or that place to hide; you've put together a psychological profile of that person to figure out how they think and therefore where'd they hide; you've had all these clever ideas; but the thing is, you're getting it wrong and you still haven't found them! Eventually the person comes out and shows themselves. How could you then boast about all those theories you worked out? They all failed! So it is with us and God: we can meditate and philosophize about God as much as we want, but we can't and won't find him until he reveals his wisdom to us through his Spirit.

This leads Paul into a discussion of who is the truly spiritual person in the Corinthian church family. The Corinthians have been deluded into thinking that wise and clever words are a sign of spiritual maturity. Paul, however, points out that the spiritual person is the one who accepts the things that come from the Spirit of God—i.e. the gospel of Christ crucified (questions 6 and 7). Therefore the spiritual person cannot be judged by the wisdom of man, since the wisdom of man cannot comprehend or grasp the hidden wisdom of God.

All of this has important implications for the divisions within the Corinthian church family. Why create divisions out of issues of human wisdom when human wisdom plays no part in knowing God? In addition, the very existence of divisions which are based on human cleverness only reflects how unspiritual they are. Because of these things, the "we" of verse 16 is best interpreted as a reference to the apostles (questions 8 and 9).

4. LEADERSHIP IN GOD'S CHURCH

1 Corinthians 3

▶ Remember: 60/40/20

 ## Getting started

Since the beginning of 1 Corinthians, we've seen that a major problem in the Corinthian church is the existence of divisive factions. So far, Paul has responded by arguing that the Corinthians have not understood the nature of the gospel. Leadership styles do not save people; only the message of the gospel (Studies 1 and 2) and the work of the Holy Spirit (Study 3) can bring people into God's kingdom. When you understand these things, divisiveness over leadership is nonsense.

But Paul is not finished with this topic yet. Not only have the Corinthians misunderstood the nature of the gospel and the role of the Spirit, they have also misunderstood what Christian leadership is all about. Paul turns to this topic in chapter 3. This is why the 'Getting started' question is designed to help people consider the topic of leadership and, in particular, what constitutes a good leader.

Studying the passage

Paul opens this section by describing the Corinthians as "infants in Christ" (v. 1). He uses this description because infants are undiscerning and don't understand what's best for them. For example, babies will just put anything in their mouths because they don't understand what's good for them and what's not. In the same way, the Corinthians are undiscerning and ignorant of which things really matter; they don't understand God's value system.

The Corinthians' immaturity is reflected in their arguing and their jealousy over positions of authority. They think that these positions make some people more important than others. However, their arguing simply betrays the extent of their worldliness, for it is the way of the world to chase after leadership in order to gain power and influence (question 1).

Paul moves to counter this worldly view of leadership with a godly view. He achieves this using three metaphors.

Image 1: A servant

In verse 5, Paul describes Christian leaders as servants. The word 'servant' here evokes the image of someone who waits on your table (question 2). The metaphor emphasizes that church leadership is about serving, not status; Christian leadership is about making things as easy and as helpful as possible so a church can grow in maturity of faith (question 3).

Image 2: A gardener

The Christian leader is also like a gardener (vv. 6-7; question 4). The emphasis here is twofold: it reflects the team nature of leadership (v. 6) while at the same time emphasizing that it is ultimately God who deserves the credit for any growth. In this respect, Paul and Apollos (for example) are simply fellow workers who each have a part to play. But only God deserves the praise (question 5).

Image 3: A builder

Paul's final image (or metaphor) is that of a builder (v. 9ff; question 6). The emphasis here is on the care with which the work must be done, for the builder will be held accountable for the quality of his work (vv. 12-15). The lesson is that church leaders are not authorities unto themselves; they are answerable to God. If what they have built survives the test of God's scrutiny, they will receive a reward. The actual nature of this reward is not explained, though it is quite possibly the wonderful joy of seeing those whom you have laboured for in the new creation (cf. 1 Thess 2:19-20). On this point, it is worth noting that Jesus Christ is the only foundation upon which the work can be built (v. 11). Paul cannot imagine any work of eternal significance or value which has not been firmly grounded in the gospel of the cross of Christ (see Study 2).

Paul's discussion of God's scrutiny of his work leads naturally into his description of the Corinthian church as "God's temple" (v. 16ff). Given the pastoral situation that Paul was responding to, this is his big point—the climax of his argument (hopefully this will be drawn out by questions 8-10). The Corinthians are fixated on leadership and roles within the church, but the real thing of value and importance is the church herself! Paul's point is quite a rebuke: to cause divisions in a church is to damage something incredibly precious to God (v. 17).

To finish

Reflection on this passage (with the 'To finish' question) should therefore lead us to value church as God values church. We should view our ministries (whatever they are) in a balanced way. Our church ministries are significant and valuable because they are performed in a community of people whom God greatly loves. But we should never make the mistake of thinking that our service gives us extra status. What more status could we possibly desire than to simply be a part of God's sacred temple in which his Spirit dwells?

5. FAITHFULNESS IN GOD'S CHURCH

1 Corinthians 4

▶ Remember: 60/40/20

 Getting started

So far, the Apostle Paul has had a lot to say about divisions and quarrelling within the Corinthian church. In the last study, Paul addressed the problem by arguing that Christian leadership needs to be understood from the proper perspective. Amongst other things, Paul pointed out that Christian leadership is about humbly serving the church, giving credit to God for any growth and realizing that leaders will have to answer to God for the quality of their work.

This understanding of leadership leads Paul into a discussion about the faithfulness or truthworthiness of church leaders. The 'Getting started' question is designed to raise some personal reflection on the challenges of being faithful to God.

Studying the passage

The chapter has two main sections. In the opening verses Paul explains the importance of faithfulness, and then in the rest of the chapter he spells out some of the implications of this lesson for the Corinthian situation.

a) Faithfulness affirmed (vv. 1-7)

Paul opens the chapter by summarizing much of his argument so far. Servanthood and the secret things of God have both already been mentioned in previous chapters. Paul has depicted himself (and Apollos and Peter) as servants who have been entrusted with the message of the cross (3:5). People are saved by the power of

God through this message. Paul now emphasizes that such a ministry requires faithfulness or trustworthiness (v. 2; question 2). Whatever the results, what matters to God is that his servants are trustworthy and committed to the task given them.

In verses 3-7, Paul presses this point by emphasizing that since it is God's judgement which matters most (question 3), the Corinthian church is wrong to elevate different people over others. In verse 6, the encouragement to "learn by us not to go beyond what is written" is probably a reference to using God's word and God's word alone as the measure of people. This has been the Corinthian problem all along; they have valued style and eloquence over faithfulness. They have therefore taken things far beyond what God considers to be important (questions 4 and 5).

b) Faithfulness applied (vv. 8-21)

To ensure that the Corinthians understand the importance of faithfulness in ministry, Paul now uses irony to describe both himself and the Corinthian church. In worldly terms, the Corinthians may have seemed wise, strong and honoured, while Paul appeared weak, foolish and dishonoured. This, however, does not take into account God's perspective. To God, Paul's poverty and lowliness are, in fact, the very marks of his success! They testify to his faithfulness in preaching the gospel without fear or favour (vv. 8-13; question 6).

But Paul does not want the Corinthian church to misunderstand his use of irony. Paul is not carelessly mocking them; he is lovingly correcting them. Paul wants nothing but the best for his precious church at Corinth, and so he calls on them to imitate him in being faithful to the gospel, irrespective of what it brings them (Questions 7 and 8).

 To finish

This study brings to a close Paul's response to the divisiveness and quarrelling within the Corinthian church. The amount of space that Paul spends on the matter is an indication of the seriousness of the problem. The 'To finish' question is designed to help round off this issue and bring closure before moving on to a different topic in the next study. This may be a good opportunity to reflect once again on the great value that God places on his church, and therefore the seriousness with which God treats anything that threatens its unity and harmony (3:16-17).

6. JUDGEMENT IN GOD'S CHURCH

1 Corinthians 5:1-6:8

▶ Remember: 60/40/20

 ## Getting started

This section marks a significant change in 1 Corinthians. Up until this point, Paul has been concerned with the problem of divisiveness and quarrelling within the church. He now turns to a second problem within the church: sexual immorality. This issue will take centre stage until the end of chapter 6. (Note that despite the apparent diversity of issues addressed in 1 Corinthians 6-7, the linking theme is that of sexual immorality—for example, compare 5:1 to 6:18-20.) The 'Getting started' question is therefore designed to draw people's attention to this change of topic. It would also be helpful to lay the foundation for the group of the idea that God is concerned about our sexuality because of his love for us. Sexual immorality is an incredibly destructive force because it goes against God's intended model for good relationships.

Studying the passage

Question 1 draws attention to the change in topic within 1 Corinthians. Paul now addresses a particularly unpleasant example of sexual immorality within the Corinthian church. A man is having a sexual relationship with his father's wife. Most assume that the woman is the man's stepmother and not his biological mother, otherwise Paul would have said "mother", rather than "father's wife". Alternatively, it may be that the matter is so unsavoury that Paul cannot bring himself to express it fully. Whatever the exact situation, it is blatant immorality which Paul says would make even the pagans baulk.

The matter is further compounded by the fact that some within the Corinthian church are proud of such immorality (question 2). To us this may seem incredible, but it may also reflect a way of thinking within the church that what we do with our bodies doesn't matter as long as we keep our minds pure. (This issue will be addressed in the next study.) Paul, however, is of the opinion that the church ought to be in mourning (v. 2) because a spiritual death has occurred. The offender should be expelled from the church (question 3). Paul offers three reasons why this is necessary.

Reason 1 (questions 4-5)
The first reason Paul gives for removing the offender from the fellowship of the church is so that he might return to Jesus (v. 5). This is a very important way of viewing church discipline. It should never be done in a high-handed self-righteous way; church discipline, like all discipline, is an act of love.

Reason 2 (questions 6-7)
By using the image of leaven (i.e. yeast) working through dough (v. 6), Paul seems to be suggesting that the offender should also be removed from the church so that his corrupting influence will not spread. Bad company corrupts, so if someone is blatantly uninterested in seeking sexual purity, they must be removed for the sake of the rest.

Reason 3 (questions 8-9)
Our English Bibles are a little unhelpful because they interrupt Paul's logic with a chapter break. In 5:12-6:8, Paul offers a third reason for disciplining the immoral one in their midst: Christ's church has, in fact, a future role to play as judges.

In 6:2, Paul points out that "the saints will judge the world". This is a tantalising verse. Usually the Bible stresses that Christ is the judge, but here we're told that somehow we Christians will also be involved in that judgement. Perhaps we will have a part to play in the judgement of this world because people will be implicated in the way they have treated God's people and his messengers (e.g. Matthew 25:31-46). Or perhaps in the new heaven and the new earth we will be able to rule over and judge creation in the same way as before the Fall.

Whatever the specifics, Paul's point is clear: the saints will be involved in judgement. This truth is relevant because if the saints have that sort of awesome responsibility, why aren't the Corinthians disciplining the immoral ones within their own church? Why aren't they exercising their role as judges?

In this context, Paul also mentions that the members of the Corinthian church are taking each other to court (6:1ff). This again reflects their failure to recognize their role as judges of the world. The irony is not lost on Paul: here is a group of people who will judge the world. Yet they are either refusing to judge when judgement is required (as with the immoral person), or they are handing over the responsibility of judging internal matters to those external to the church (i.e. they are allowing the world to be their judge!).

To finish

When drawing together the themes of this study, it is important to remind your group that the central theme is that of sexual immorality within the church. This theme emphasizes what Paul has already repeatedly pointed out to the Corinthians: God's church is a very precious community. Therefore, just as divisiveness within the church needs to be treated very seriously, so too does sexual immorality. This is especially critical because the saints will judge the world. So how can we refrain from judging immorality within ourselves?

7. PURITY IN GOD'S CHURCH

1 Corinthians 6:9-20

▶ Remember: 60/40/20

 Getting started

In the last study, we saw Paul switching topics in order to deal with a particularly unpleasant incident of sexual immorality. So far, he has offered three reasons why this matter is so serious that the offender should be expelled from the church:

Reason 1: So that offender might repent;

Reason 2: So that immorality might not spread to others in the church;

Reason 3: Because the saints have a role to play in judgement.

In this study, Paul advances a fourth reason: because we should honour God with our bodies. The 'Getting started' question introduces this topic by stimulating discussion about how our thoughts and actions are linked.

Studying the passage

Corinth's reputation for sexual promiscuity and degeneracy was legendary all over the ancient world. In the opening verses of this section, Paul wants to emphasize that such immorality should be a thing of the past for Christians. Through the gospel of Jesus Christ, the Corinthian Christians are now pure, holy and guiltless before God—washed, sanctified and justified in the name of Jesus and by the Spirit of God (v. 11). As a consequence, they ought to be pure and holy in the way they live (questions 1-2).

With this in mind, Paul now stresses that our identity in Christ affects what we do with our bodies. At the time of his writing, many believed in the common philosophical idea that what we do with our bodies doesn't actually affect us spiritually. Some in the ancient world thought that the physical world was so different to the spiritual world, we could do anything on a physical level and it would be irrelevant spiritually.

For this reason, the statement, "All things are lawful for me" (v. 12) is probably best taken as a quote from some of the Corinthians in the church who felt that they were above moral rules and that their bodies had nothing to do with their spiritual lives. In the same way, "Food is meant for the stomach and the stomach for food" is probably also a slogan for those who thought that since God is going to destroy the physical world, what we do physically doesn't matter. Such thinking implies that since the body is for sex and sex is for the body, sexual immorality is of no consequence since both will be destroyed in the end.

Paul, however, wants to rectify this misunderstanding. All things may be lawful but not everything is helpful (v. 12; question 3) because:

1. the body was not made for immorality (v. 13); and

2. the body is not destined for destruction but for resurrection (v. 14; question 4).

Therefore we must conclude that what we do with our bodies matters. This is especially true for sexual activity, since the sexual union is such an intimate act. For this reason, Paul finds it incomprehensible that a member of Christ's body (i.e. a member of Christ's church) would unite himself with a prostitute. To unite with Christ means that we do not unite with others in sexual immorality (questions 5 and 6).

The intimacy of sexual activity also leads Paul to observe that "Every other sin a person commits is outside the body, but the sexually immoral person sins against his own body" (v. 18). This is a difficult verse to understand. At the very least, it is saying that sexual sins are in a different category to other sins. It's not that they are worse, but they are definitely different. Presumably this is because sexual intimacy influences so much of our personal identity and self-worth. This is why God intended sexual intimacy to be a special act reserved for the most intimate and secure of relationships. It is also why sexual immorality has such capacity for devastation. Sex is not like eating. Because our sexuality is such a deep part of who we are, there are very few sins as destructive as sexual immorality (question 7).

Question 9 concludes the 'Light from the Word' section by reminding us of the context of Paul's comments: the topic of sexual immorality has arisen because of a problem within the church (1 Cor 5:1). In our last study, we looked at three reasons why this problem is so serious that it ought to be addressed through church discipline. This study has highlighted a fourth reason why the problem is so serious: sexual immorality is inconsistent behaviour for a follower of Jesus Christ. Christians have been washed, sanctified and justified; they are members of Christ's body, the church; and they will one day be raised with Christ himself. For these reasons, followers of Jesus should honour God with their bodies.

8. GODLINESS IN GOD'S CHURCH

1 Corinthians 7

▶ Remember: 60/40/20

 ## Getting started

We live in a society confused about its attitude to singleness and marriage. On the one hand, being single is to live in the land of the free; you are able to do whatever you want without being stifled by others. We see this on television all the time, and now more and more shows revolve around groups of friends instead of married couples and families. On the other hand, movies like *Sleepless in Seattle* depict singleness as being sad and lonely. Marriage is a thing to strive for, and having a partner means enjoyment, fulfilment and romance. The 'Getting started' question invites people to discuss their attitudes to marriage and singleness, as it is this topic to which the Apostle Paul now turns.

Studying the passage

We have reached another important turning point in the letter. The two topics before this (divisiveness and sexual immorality) were raised at Paul's initiative. But now Paul starts to address topics which the Corinthians themselves have raised (v. 1; question 1).

This means that a degree of caution is required when approaching the text. No doubt Paul shaped his response according to the question he was originally asked (question 2). This chapter also contains several verses and words whose meanings are highly debatable. In addition, the issues he raises (marriage, singleness, divorce and separation) are highly emotive and may be painful for some in your group. So approach this study in a sensitive and loving way. (Note that because of these things, this study is perhaps the most directed of them all.) We will examine the text under the headings of Paul's three main truths.

Truth 1: Marriage is good

In 1 Corinthians 7:1-16, Paul addresses those in the church who already have had some experience of marriage. (Taking this reading, "the unmarried" in verse 8 is probably a reference to male widowers. There isn't a specific term for them in the New Testament.)

In this passage, Paul defends marriage as good because it provides an appropriate relationship for sex. This sounds too clinical to us. Where's the romance? Perhaps we've been influenced too much by Hollywood's desire for romance and not influenced enough by God's desire for holiness.

Note the context of the problem of sexual immorality in the church in the previous chapters. Paul is not saying that sex is the *only* reason for marriage. But it is certainly a valid reason for marriage, especially given Corinthian culture and society.

The context of immorality within the church of God also explains why Paul spends time expounding how sexual passion is meant to be expressed in a God-honouring way within marriage. Because we are to honour God with our bodies (see previous study), sex is therefore not to be used selfishly (vv. 3-4). Furthermore, since the sexual union is an expression of the oneness of marriage, marriage should be seen as a permanent commitment (v. 10ff; questions 3 and 4). Even being married to an unbeliever is not a valid excuse to initiate divorce (vv. 12-13).

Truth 2: Singleness is good

In 1 Corinthians 7:25, Paul turns to his attention to those who have not yet had any experience of marriage. Paul defends the goodness of singleness as it enables a person to be less distracted in the pursuit of the Lord's affairs (vv. 32-35; question 5). Paul's thinking behind the advantages of singleness seems to be particularly motivated by "the present distress" (v. 26). It is unclear exactly what this "present distress" is: it could refer to sexual immorality within the church (and therefore Paul is keen for as many as possible to have self-control in the area of sexuality) or it might refer to persecution. In the light of verses 29-31, the latter interpretation is seen by most as more likely (question 6). Whatever the specifics, Paul's point is still clear: singleness is good because it allows one to live with "undivided devotion to the Lord" (v. 35).

Truth 3: Remain in your situation

The key lesson of the chapter is nestled in the middle of Paul's teaching about marriage and singleness. In verses 17-24, Paul explains that we shouldn't be fixated on our life circumstances. Whatever they may be, what matters most is seeking to be godly (question 8). Paul applies and illustrates this "rule" using circumcision and slavery (question 9), but it is also a rule which makes sense of all that Paul has stated elsewhere in the chapter about marriage and singleness. Paul's main point is that each has its advantages: being married helps our godliness by satisfying our sexual desires, and being single helps our godliness by allowing us to remain undivided in our devotion to the Lord. In the end, external circumstances don't matter; "keeping the commandments of God" is what counts (v. 19; question 10).

To finish

The finishing question is designed to help flesh out the implications of Paul's central lesson in verses 17-24. Often we excuse our lukewarm attitude to Jesus by blaming our circumstances. We say things like, "If only there weren't the family pressures, I'd be able to spend more time in prayer", or "If only work wasn't so hectic, I'd be able to get along to Bible study group more often", or "If only I was married, I'd be able to do really great things for the Lord". 1 Corinthians 7 is saying that all of those things are not true: the problem is not our life situation—the problem is us. Paul therefore encourages the Corinthians to stop focusing on their life situation and to simply get on with doing what God says—whatever that may be.

matthiasmedia

Matthias Media is a ministry team of like-minded, evangelical Christians working together to achieve a particular goal, as summarized in our mission statement:

To serve our Lord Jesus Christ, and the growth of his gospel in the world, by producing and delivering high quality, Bible-based resources.

It was in 1988 that we first started pursuing this mission together, and in God's kindness we now have more than 250 different ministry resources being distributed all over the world. These resources range from Bible studies and books, through to training courses and audio sermons.

To find out more about our large range of very useful products, and to access samples and free downloads, visit our website:

www.matthiasmedia.com.au

How to purchase our resources

1 Through a range of outlets in various parts of the world: visit **www.matthiasmedia.com.au/contact/overseas.htm** for details about recommended retailers in your part of the world.

2 Direct from us over the internet:
  – in the US: www.matthiasmedia.com
  – in Australia and the rest of the world: www.matthiasmedia.com.au

3 Direct from us by phone:
  – within Australia: 1800 814 360 (Sydney: 9663 1478)
  – international: +61-2-9663-1478

4 Trade enquiries worldwide:
  – email us: sales@matthiasmedia.com.au